A TUDOR WARSHIP

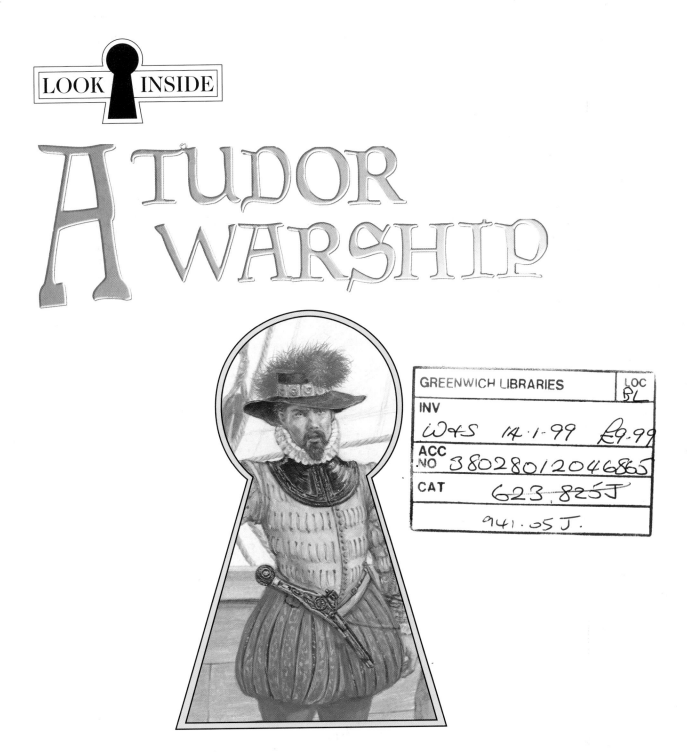

BRIAN MOSES
Illustrated by Adam Hook

WAYLAND

Editor: Jason Hook
Designer: Ian Winton/Heather Blackham
Cover: Dennis Day

First published in 1998 by Wayland Publishers Ltd,
61 Western Road, Hove, East Sussex, BN3 1JD, England

Find Wayland on the Internet at
http://www.wayland.co.uk

British Library Cataloguing in Publication Data
   Moses, Brian, 1950-
   Look inside a Tudor warship
   1. Warships - England - History - 16th century -
   Juvenile literature
   I. Title II. Hook, Adam III. A Tudor Warship
   359.8'32'0942'09031

ISBN 0 7502 1957 2

Production controller: Carol Titchener
Colour reproduction by Page Turn, Hove, England
Printed and bound in Italy by G. Canale & CSpA, Turin

Cover Pictures: The *Mary Rose* (centre); a cannon
from the *Mary Rose* (top); a compass (left);
a quadrant (right).

Picture Acknowledgements: The publishers would like to thank the
following for permission to publish their pictures: (t=top; c=centre;
b=bottom; l=left; r=right) Ashmolean Museum 19br; Bodleian
Library 27t; Bridgeman Art Library /Pepys Library, Magdalene
College, Cambridge 4t, /Master and Fellows, Magdalene College,
Cambridge 6c, /National Maritime Museum 10t, 18b, /British Library
21tr, /Stadelsches Kunstinstitut, Frankfurt-am-Main 25tl, /Victoria &
Albert Museum 26t, /Wallace Collection 27b; British Library 13l, 20-
1(details); Getty Images 17c; Mary Rose Trust 6t, 7t, 10b, 10c, 11br,
12b, 12l, 13tr, 14b, 19tl, 22t, 23tr, 24t, 25bl, 25br, 29tl, 29tr; Master
and Fellows, Magdalene College, Cambridge *cover* (c), 7b, 15t;
Michael Holford *cover* (bl, br, b/g), 17t, 18t, 20t; National Maritime
Museum *cover* (t), 8t, 9b, 11l, 14t, 16t, 20b, 21b, 26b, 28t, 28b;
Oxford Scientific Films 13br, 15b; Photri, Courtesy of the John
Carter Brown Library at Brown University 14c, 23l; Royal Collection
Enterprises ©Her Majesty The Queen 4b; Science and Society 8b,
17b; Ulster Museum 6b, 11t, 16b, 19bl, 30, 31.

All quotes are credited on page 31.

CONTENTS

SHIP

AT THE DOCKS

Take a look aboard a Tudor warship. Through the main hatch, sailors load barrels of water, vinegar, beer and salted beef; straw mattresses; charts and instruments; cannon balls and longbows. A ship's boy leans on his mop and watches. Not for the first time, he wonders why he ever wanted to run away to sea.

▼ Henry VIII embarks from Dover on the *Great Harry* in 1520.

▶ A model of Henry VIII's warship, the *Great Harry*.

In the sixteenth century, docks like Portsmouth were busy places. Wagonloads of wood arrived daily for the many new warships being built. The best shipwrights were paid sixpence a day for their skills. They also received board and lodging, but had to sleep three to a bed.

A Spanish official said in 1588: 'The sea is so full of English ships, for the English have become the lords and masters of the sea and care for no man else.'[1]

4

Warships, or 'galleons', built to defend England during the reign of King Henry VIII (1509-1547), were little more than floating gun platforms. Henry's finest ship, the *Great Harry*, could carry 100 cannon. Another of his ships, the *Mary Rose*, was loaded with bronze and iron guns when she sank near Portsmouth in 1545.

'To pass the seas some think a toil,
Some think it strange abroad to roam,
Some think it grief to leave their soil,
Their parents, kinfolk, and their home.
Think so who list, I like it not:
I must abroad to try my lot.'[3]

In 1588, Spain sent an Armada of over one hundred ships to try to invade England. By this time, English warships had become faster and easier to manoeuvre. Under the command of the great captains of the day, the English fleet won a famous victory.

▼ A cutaway view of a Tudor warship.

aftercastle
bonaventure mast
mizzen mast
foremast
forecastle
poop deck
quarterdeck
mainmast
bowsprit
weather deck
stern
heads
captain's cabin
bows
tiller
gun-decks
rudder
keel
stores
hold
galley
ballast
bilges

HULL

THE SHIPWRIGHTS

Peering into the carpenter's cabin, the ship's boy sees two finely dressed men studying drawings of the ship. One uses a pair of dividers to check the measurements of the keel. Yesterday, the boy helped the ship's carpenter to repair old timbers down in the hold. He hates it there. It's dark, the stench is awful and there are rats and cockroaches everywhere.

▲ These dividers, from the *Mary Rose*, were used by the ship's navigator.

▲ Tudor shipwrights using dividers to draw up plans.

The hull was the main body of the ship. A keel of oak or elm was the 'backbone' around which curved timbers called 'ribs' were fixed. Decks, supporting beams and side-planks were added next. Rope dipped in tar was then hammered between the planks to make them watertight. This was called 'caulking'. A coating of pitch and goat's hair was mistakenly believed to keep off worms and barnacles.

In the bilges, at the very bottom of the hull, ships carried ballast. This was made up of rocks, gravel and sometimes cannon balls, and helped the ship to stay upright. Seawater which seeped into the ship lay in the bilges and mixed with rats' droppings. It smelt terrible and had to be pumped out.

▲ Ballast used by a ship of the Armada.

The design of the warship's hull was based on the shape of a fish. The keel was rounded like a cod's head at the bows and narrowed to a thinner, streamlined stern like a mackerel's tail. One captain noted that every warship was a different size, because shipwrights would rather trust 'their eye than their scale and compass'.[5]

Departed from Gravesend on the 12th May 1557 ...

weighed anchor and plied down the Thames. Wind easterly.[4]

▼ Tools used by the carpenter on the *Mary Rose*.

'The carpenter ... is the man who gives life to the ship ... all the works that iron or timber is used in, pass through his hands and skill. He looks to the hull of the ship, that there be no damage by leaks within board or without.'[6]

▼ Elizabeth I's shipwright, Matthew Baker, designed this hull to look like a fish.

SAILS

IN THE RIGGING

As they reach open sea, the ship's boy is ordered to climb up the mainmast. High in the rigging, a fierce wind gusts through the canvas. He tries to untie a rope holding the sails, but his fingers are not strong enough. Suddenly, the boy is elbowed aside, and he almost loses grip of the rigging. He feels sick as he looks down and sees how far he might have fallen.

▲ Sailors climb the rigging of a Portugese ship.

The ship's sails were made of canvas strips called cloths. These were sewn together and the edges strengthened with rope. Sails were raised and lowered using the 'rigging' – a network of pulleys, lines and pins.

Men clambered high into the masts to adjust the canvas, as you can see in the painting above. They found footholds in 'rat-lines', which were pieces of rope dipped in tar and fixed to the rigging.

*'To my God let us pray, to make safe our way,
And His Mother, Our Lady, who prays for us all,
To save us from tempest and threatening squall.'*[7]

◀ This model shows the rigging of an English warship, in 1600.

◀ The ship's boy mending a sail.

The piercing cold of the gross, thick air will so stiffen and fur the sail and ship tackling that no mariner can either hoist or strike them.[8]

When a lookout high in the topcastle saw storm clouds approaching, the order was given to shorten the sails. High winds could tear the canvas to pieces and break the masts. Sailors had to climb the rigging while the ship was lurching from side to side. Lives were lost when men were torn from their perches and tossed into the rough seas.

▲ A painting showing the sails and pennants of the English and Spanish fleets, in 1588.

CAPTAIN

A LIFE OF LUXURY

Carrying in the captain's supper, the ship's boy finds himself staring wide-eyed at a large cabin with glass windows and comfortable furniture. The table is set with pewter spoons, and a musician is playing a pipe. The boy sets the meal down, wishing that he could help himself to the bacon, dried fruit, marmalade and sugar.

▶ Sir John Hawkins, one of the great sea captains.

▲ Pewter dinner ware from the *Mary Rose*.

Other captains were experienced 'merchant adventurers'. Sir John Hawkins began his career as a slave trader and pirate, raiding Spanish ships in the Caribbean. He rose to become Treasurer of the Navy, where he worked to improve English ships and conditions on board them. Sir John also commanded a ship in the battle against the Armada.

Sometimes, the ship's captain was a gentleman who knew very little about sailing. He did know how a gentleman should behave, though, and expected his life to be as comfortable at sea as it was on land. The captain dined at a cloth-covered table, waited on by servants. Items on the *Mary Rose* included pewter plates, tankards, and a manicure set used to file an officer's nails.

◀ An officer's manicure set, made of bone.

Also found on the *Mary Rose* were embroidered leather purses, fine velvet trimmings, satin-covered buttons and a pomander which held sweet-smelling herbs. All these items show how officers enjoyed a very different life to the ordinary men on board.

'Serve God daily, love one another, preserve your victuals, beware of fire and keep good company.'

▲ Gold buttons worn by an officer of the Armada.

A pewter chamber pot found on the *Mary Rose* shows that officers preferred to make their own toilet arrangements, rather than join the queue for the 'heads'. These were boxes with holes cut in them. They were positioned behind the decorated 'beakhead' at the front of the ship. Whatever sailors did there, went straight over the side!

▲ Lord Howard of Effingham commanded the English fleet against the Armada.

◄ A captain's chamber pot from the *Mary Rose*.

Despite having the most luxurious accommodation on the ship, one officer described his cabin as, 'A thing much like to some gentleman's dog kennel.'

SAILORS

BELOW DECK

After a 'watch' of four hours, the lad is sent below decks. Some men have hammocks, but he 'planks it' – sleeping on the cramped, hard deck with rats scuttling past him. He tries to remember when he last had a wash. He knows that he smells and that everyone else does too. He feels tired all the time and worries that he will fall ill. Already there are cuts all over his hands from pulling on the ropes.

▶ A sailor in his hammock.

▲ Gold coins from the *Mary Rose*.

Sailors preferred to voyage with merchant ships, where there was less discipline and more chance of looting treasure. But the Royal Navy kept a record of skilled sailors. Before the Armada battle, sailors on a register in Ipswich were paid three shillings and ordered to report to Her Majesty Queen Elizabeth I's ships.

There was no uniform on board the warship. An assortment of leather shoes were found on the *Mary Rose*, ranging from simple slippers to knee-length boots. Some sailors went barefoot. They found that this gave them a better grip on wet decks and rigging.

▶ Leather shoes worn by sailors on board the *Mary Rose*.

If you looked below the warship's decks you would see sailors wearing simple, sleeveless leather jerkins and baggy knee breeches. Many wore belts holding an embroidered pouch and dagger. The more elegant among them wore coats of green-and-white stripes, and silk-lined, fur hats.

He is a lewd and seditious fellowe, naughty and bad and his father is a witch.

I think he comes from the devil himself.[10]

Most voyages suffered loss of life through accident and illness. Rats were a major problem. Over 40,000 were recorded on one ship. They chewed away at spare sails, ate their way into food supplies and spread disease. Ships also swarmed with lice, fleas, bedbugs and cockroaches.

◀ A sailor's possessions from the *Mary Rose*.

▲ Sailors wore baggy trousers and fur hats when going on shore leave.

▶ Rats chewed through the ship's rigging.

'No kinds of men of any profession in the commonwealth passe their years in so great and continual hazard ... and ... of so many so few grow to grey haires.'[11]

BISCUIT

THE GALLEY

The ship's boy sips some beer. It is sour but he has to drink something. All the water they brought on board has turned green with dirt and scum. He is hungry all the time, but before he can eat the hard ship's biscuit he has to knock it on the table to get rid of the wriggling weevils.

▲ Ship's biscuit.

▲ Sixteenth-century sailors loading the stores.

RATIONS

Sundays, Tuesdays, Thursdays: 900 g salted beef, 450 g biscuit, 4.5 litres beer.

Mondays: 450 g ham, 0.5 litres peas, 450 g biscuit, 4.5 litres beer.

Wednesdays, Fridays, Saturdays: 1/4 dried cod, 330 g cheese, 330 g butter, 450 g biscuit, 4.5 litres beer.

For a four-month voyage, the meat of one cow was loaded for every crew member. The stores also held a good supply of salted pork, cod, dried peas and biscuit. But the Tudors knew very little about food hygiene. Meat went bad. Cheese and flour became maggoty.

Water barrels always leaked or were fouled by rats. On long voyages, rainwater had to be collected by hanging mats on the rigging and collecting the drips. Some men even drank their own urine.

◀ Utensils from the *Mary Rose*.

Food was cooked in copper cauldrons over a brick firebox in the ship's kitchen, which was called the 'galley'. The stink from bilges full of seawater and rats' droppings was very strong here. The taste of bad food was disguised with vinegar. Some sailors brought their own spices to improve the flavour.

Victuals were so scarce that we were driven to eat hides, cats, rats, parrots, monkeys and dogs.[12]

◄ The *Mary Rose*, with a list of its equipment.

'*We ate only old biscuit reduced to powder, and full of grubs, and stinking from the dirt which the rats had made on it ... We also ate the ox-hides ... the sawdust of wood, and rats.*'[13]

◄ Rats ate and fouled the ship's precious stores.

Sailors on long voyages ate very few fresh fruits and vegetables. Because of this, many suffered from a terrible disease called scurvy which is caused by a lack of Vitamin C. Not until the 1700s was it realised that oranges, lemons and limes could prevent scurvy. Up to 10,000 sailors died from the disease during the reign of Queen Elizabeth I, from 1558 to 1603.

One sailor described the suffering caused by scurvy: 'It rotted all my gums, which gave out a stinking black blood. My thighs and lower legs were black and gangrenous.'[14]

LATITUDE AND LONGITUDE

The navigator tries to take a reading using his backstaff. Although the sun is shining, it is very windy and the sea is rough. He holds the long instrument up to his eye, and stumbles about on the unsteady deck. It takes him several attempts to sight the sun with the pointer, until at last he is happy with the reading.

The navigator needed to work out the ship's 'latitude', its position north or south of the equator. He knew that at noon the sun was directly overhead at the equator, and lower in the sky the further north or south a ship travelled. If he measured the sun's height above the horizon at noon, the navigator could calculate his latitude.

◀ This astrolabe guided the Armada to England's shores.

▶ A navigator using a backstaff.

Different instruments were used to measure the sun's height. A brass 'astrolabe' was hung by a cord and its pointer rotated towards the sun. A metre-long pole called a 'cross-staff' had a sliding bar which the navigator lined up between the horizon and the sun. He then checked his readings against charts and tables.

◀ This instrument, made in 1543, was used to navigate at night.

To use an astrolabe or cross-staff, the poor navigator had to stare directly into the sun's glare. This problem was solved by English navigator John Davis, who invented the backstaff in 1594. Navigators, like the one on the opposite page, could now measure latitude with their backs to the sun.

◀ An astronomer using navigational instruments.

Time was measured using the ship's sand-glass. This had to be turned over every two hours, like a giant egg-timer. Without a more accurate clock, Tudor navigators could not measure 'longitude', a ship's position to east or west. Many ships simply travelled to the latitude of their destination, then sailed east or west until land was sighted.

▶ This astrolabe from 1558 measured the position of the stars.

FINDING DIRECTION

A sailor throws a log over the side, attached to a line tied with knots. His comrade turns over a sand-glass. They count how many knots are fed out before the sand runs through the glass, and so try to work out the ship's speed.

> 'One glass has gone, another's a-filling,
> More sand shall run, if God is willing.'[16]

To steer a course across huge oceans, where no landmarks could be seen, the Tudor navigator relied on a system called 'dead reckoning'. The first stage was to check the compass, and work out the exact direction the ship was sailing in.

▲ A sixteenth-century sand-glass.

Next, the navigator worked out the speed of the ship. He either used the log and line, or watched to see how quickly seaweed floated past. Finally, he measured time with a sand-glass. Knowing the speed, direction and time of the voyage, the navigator used dividers and a protractor to plot the ship's course on to a chart.

▲ Sir Francis Drake's compass also measured latitude and tides.

> 'When you come to have sight of any coast or land ... set the same with your sailing compass ... noting your judgement how far you think it from you, drawing also the form of it in your book.'[17]

The first sailing compasses were needles that had been magnetized. These swung round to point north when suspended on a string. By Tudor times, compass needles were mounted on card and balanced on a central point. Some compasses, like the one below, were kept in wooden boxes, which made the magnetic needle far more accurate.

A great storm struck us that night, which lasted until the middle of next day, which necessitated our lifting anchor and letting ourselves drift hither and thither about the bay.[18]

◀ A compass from the *Mary Rose*.

Some captains kept a journal of the compass readings, progress and important events of their voyage. Because this journal included a record of the ship's speed, as measured by throwing the log overboard, it became known as the ship's 'log'.

▶ A compass used on a ship of the Armada.

▲ Edward Fiennes, the Lord High Admiral, holding a compass in 1562.

CHARTS

PLOTTING A COURSE

The wind suddenly changes, blowing the ship eastwards. The helmsman, who steers the ship, marks the new direction by placing a peg in a board. This 'traverse board' has lines of holes running towards each compass point. The pegs in each line show how far the ship has sailed in that direction. At the end of his watch, the helmsman counts up the pegs, and writes his course in the ship's 'log'.

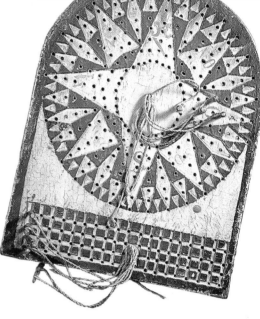

▲ A traverse board with pegs showing the ship's progress to the east.

There were different types of chart for navigating coasts and oceans. To safely sail around a coast, captains used notebooks called 'rutters'. These were filled with navigators' notes describing depths, tides and shoals.

To map a coast, a lead and line were thrown over the side. In the end of the lead was sticky fat which picked up sand from the seabed. The line measured depth. By comparing the sand and depth with notes in his rutter, the captain could recognize different coasts. You can see sailors using a lead and line on the cover of the rutter shown on the left.

▲ A rutter called *The Mariners' Mirrour*, from 1588.

Charts for ocean voyages were less accurate. Lord Howard said of one chart, 'We find it by experience and daily observation to be an hundred miles over.'[19] Even when Gerard Mercator published the first accurate chart in 1569, many sailors preferred to rely on their old astrolabes.

'I could wish all seamen would give over sailing by the false plain charts, and sail by Mercator's chart, which is according to the truth of navigation.'[20]

There is 100 or 150 fathoms of water in depth off the coast ... we saw many whales very monstrous and by estimation 60 foot long and they roared and cried terrible.[21]

▼ A navigator's chart from 1535.

▲ Warships on a map drawn in 1558.

DISCIPLINE

The toll of the ship's bell summons the whole crew on deck. The ship's boy watches in horror as a sailor who has been caught stealing is tied to the mainmast. The lad holds his ears to block out the terrible screams, as the bosun lashes the man again and again. Then, the bosun rubs salt into the sailor's bloody back. 'That'll help his wounds to heal,' one of the crew mutters, 'and teach him not to thieve.'

▲ The bell from the *Mary Rose*.

Discipline was harsh on board a Tudor warship. The sea was a dangerous place and the captain needed his crew to be both obedient and efficient. If sailors refused to obey orders or risked the safety of the ship, they were flogged.

'*Take particular care that no soldier, sailor or other person in the Armada shall blaspheme, or deny Our Lord, Our Lady, or the Saints, under very severe punishment to be inflicted at our discretion.*'[22]

A sailor was flogged on his bare back with a whip or lash called a cat-o'-nine-tails. This had nine lengths of knotted cord fixed to its wooden handle.

◀ A sailor is flogged at the mainmast.

The bosun was the officer in charge of the crew. The high-pitched sound of his whistle or 'call' was a signal to sailors that an order must be obeyed. Anyone who reacted too slowly might receive a rap from the bosun's rod. Greater threats to the captain's authority met with more severe punishments.

We must have these mutinies and discords that are grown amongst us redressed.

Let us show ourselves to be all of a company.[23]

▶ The bosun on the *Mary Rose* used this whistle or 'call'.

'Put a man in leg-irons. Withhold his food. Duck him in the water. Haul him under the keel ... Hang weights around his neck, until his 'heart' of spine begins to break. Stop up his tongue or cut a portion out of it, as a punishment for blasphemy or swearing.'[24]

A sailor who fell asleep when he should be on watch had a bucket of water thrown on his neck. If he repeated the offence four times, he was tied to the bowsprit. A murderer was bound to the corpse of his victim and thrown overboard. Thomas Doughty, a sailor who was convicted of mutiny on Sir Francis Drake's ship, was beheaded.

▲ Sir Francis Drake, dressed for battle.

FIDDLE

LEISURE

Sometimes, the ship's boy thinks that he actually likes being a sailor. The weather is fine today and the ocean is calm. Men fish from the side of the ship, or laze around playing a board game called 'nine men's morris'. The beer ration has been doubled, and one sailor dances to the music of a fiddle.

▲ Parts of a tabor, pipes and fiddles from the *Mary Rose*.

When sailors weren't on watch or sleeping below decks, they were able to snatch a few moments of leisure. They danced to the music of fiddles, lutes and tambourines. A 'tabor', or drum, and three 'tabor pipes', which were blown to accompany the drum, were found in the crew's quarters on the *Mary Rose*.

◄ Music entertained the crew at sea.

Sailors gambled with dice or cards, and listened to storytellers spin 'yarns', or stories, about the sea. When the weather was fine, the crew sat on deck and sang choruses of folk songs. The special task of the ship's boy was to sing prayers at sunrise and sunset.

A captain must forbid the lavish use of shooting for pleasure at the meeting of ships, passing by castles, and banqueting aboard. For indeed there is more powder wastefully spent in this sort than against any enemy.[25]

▼ A sixteenth-century crew enjoy a celebration.

A Sailors' Folk Song:

'As I lay musing in my bed,
Full warm and well at ease,
I thought upon the lodgings hard,
Poor sailors had at sea.
Our ship that was before so good,
And eke so likewise trim,
Is now with raging seas grown leakt,
And water fast comes in.'[26]

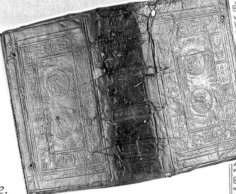

▶ A book cover from the *Mary Rose*.

▲ A backgammon board from the *Mary Rose*.

Feast days and the crossing of the equator were celebrated with beer, gunshots and rough games. Officers meanwhile relaxed with games and books. On board the *Mary Rose* were found a folded, oak backgammon set complete with all its counters, and a board for 'nine men's morris'. Book covers have also survived, showing that officers, and perhaps some of the men, were able to read.

PISTOL

WAR AT SEA

It is the first time in battle for the ship's boy, and he feels a mixture of fear and excitement. Under cover of darkness, he helps the gunners to load up a small boat with gunpowder, rope and pitch. They set this craft alight, and launch it towards the enemy.

◄ Pistols from the sixteenth century.

▲ The launch of fireships against the Armada.

Fire on board ship was a great danger, as it could easily reach the gunpowder barrels and cause a terrible explosion. During the Armada battle in 1588, fireships were loaded with explosives and sent towards the Spanish ships. These 'Hellburners' caused great confusion among the Spanish sailors as they tried desperately to escape.

Preparing fireships against the Armada, the English sailors 'filled them with gunpowder, pitch, brimstone, and with other combustible and fiery matter ... charging all their ordnance [guns] with powder, bullets and stones'.[27]

◄ English captain Sir Martin Frobisher, armed with pistol and sword, and wearing a bosun's call.

Her decks were a shambles, her guns silent, and blood was still spilling out of her scuppers.[28]

◄ Compare the hilt of this sword with the one worn by Frobisher.

In the early sixteenth century, naval battles were fought at close range. Warships were built with raised 'castles' at each end. From the height of these castles, sailors attacked an enemy crew with small cannon, pistols, exploding brass grenades and rocks. 'Fire pots' were thrown to set light to rigging. The English were also famous bowmen. Sailors and soldiers on the *Mary Rose* were armed with 250 longbows and more than 9,000 arrows.

'The ship is taken and the men at your mercy; wherein, nevertheless, a soldier-like quarter is always to be given ... never ... be bloody in cold blood, nor cruel at any time.'[29]

Grappling hooks were used to pull an enemy ship alongside. Sailors then took up their swords, pikes and bills, and led the assault. They fought desperately to board the enemy warship, and capture her as their prize.

THE THUNDER OF GUNS

The ship's boy stumbles through the smoke-filled decks, carrying orders to the gunners. His ears are filled with the thundering of the cannon and he feels faint at the sight of so much blood.

'A gunner in time of service ought to forbid with meek and courteous speeches all manner of persons, other than his appointed assistants, to come near his pieces [guns], so that none of his pieces may be choked, poisoned, or hurt.'[30]

▲ A painting of the Armada battle.

▼ A cannon from the *Mary Rose*.

By the time of the Armada battle, English warships fought in a different way. Staying at a distance, a captain sailed parallel to the enemy. He then blasted a 'broadside', firing all of the powerful cannon on one side of his ship.

The gunner loaded his cannon with a charge of gunpowder and lead or stone shot, jammed down with a long ramrod. He used wedges to line up the gun-carriage. It was difficult to be accurate, as the ship's deck rose and fell. The gunner aimed either to pierce the enemy ship's hull, or to tear away her masts and rigging.

'A gunner ought to be a sober, wakeful, lusty, hardy, patient, prudent and quick-spirited man. He ought also to have a good eyesight.'[31]

▶ A linstock from the *Mary Rose*.

The ship was marvellous unsavoury, filled with blood and bodies of dead and wounded men like a slaughterhouse.[32]

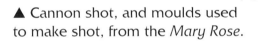

▲ Cannon shot, and moulds used to make shot, from the *Mary Rose*.

A burning match in a 'linstock' was used to light the cannon. The gun roared and the shot hurtled across the sea. Gunners wounded by enemy fire were carried away through the smoke. They were placed in the hold, among the ballast and rats, so that their screams could not be heard.

▼ The ship's boy carries a gunner's powder.

GLOSSARY

Barnacles Small sea creatures that cling to ships' bottoms, forming a rough surface.

Beakhead The long beam at the front of a ship.

Bilges The lowest area inside a ship's hull.

Bills Weapons with a hook on the end of a long pole.

Blasphemy Talking without respect about sacred things.

Bows The front of a ship.

Bowsprit A pole sticking out from the ship's bows.

Breeches Trousers fastened below the knee.

Brimstone Sulphur, a material used to make gunpowder.

Combustible Able to burn.

Dividers A measuring instrument.

Embarks Sets sail on a ship.

Equator An imaginary line around the middle of the earth.

Fathoms An old measurement of depth (1.829 metres).

Gangrenous Infected with a disease that eats away the flesh.

Jerkins Jackets without sleeves.

Lewd Rude, obscene.

Lutes Instruments similar to guitars.

Mutinies Revolts by sailors against their officers.

Pennants Flags flown by ships.

Pewter A mixture of lead and tin used for making cups and plates.

Pitch A tar-like substance used to caulk ships.

Protractor An instrument for measuring angles.

Scuppers Drains at the side of a ship's deck.

Seditious Trying to stir up rebellion.

Shipwrights Shipbuilders and ships' carpenters.

Squall A sudden, gusty storm.

Stern The rear of a ship.

Topcastle The lookout's platform at the top of the mast.

Victuals Food and drink.

Weevils Insects that damage stored grain.

FURTHER READING

BOOKS TO READ

Richard Humble and Mark Bergin, *A Sixteenth Century Galleon* (Simon & Schuster, 1993)
Rupert Matthews, *Explorer* (Dorling Kindersley, 1991)
Elizabeth Newbery, *Tudor Warship* (A & C Black, 1996)
Peter Padfield, *Armada* (Victor Gollancz, 1988)
Pam Robson, *The Spanish Armada* (Macdonald Young, 1996)
Margaret Rule, *Tudors and Stuarts, Life at Sea* (Wayland, 1994)
Mary Rose, Exhibition and Ship Hall (The Mary Rose Trust, 1997)

QUOTES

1. A Spanish official in 1588.
2. Sloane MSS, a bill for outfitting a ship in January 1587.
3. *A Ballad in Praise of Seafaring Men,* about 1585.
4. *The Calendars of State Papers,* Elizabeth R, 1558.
5. *The Jewell of Artes,* 1604.
6. Sir William Monson, Elizabethan commander, *Naval Tracts.*
7. Traditional Spanish prayer.
8. Sir Humphrey Gilbert, *Discourse of a Discovery for a New Passage to Cathay,* 1576.
9. Sir John Hawkins, 1564.
10. Captain of the ship *Elizabeth,* writing about the sailor Matthew Jonas.
11. Sir Richard Hakluyt, English chaplain and geographer, 1598.
12. Job Hortop, sailor on the *Jesus of Lubeck,* 1567.
13. Ferdinand Magellan, 1521.
14. Extract from the *Chronicle of the Voyage of Vasco da Gama,* 1498.
15. *The Calendars of State Papers.*
16. Spanish, traditional.
17. Instructions to Arthur Pet and Charles Jackman before a voyage in 1580.
18. A sailor on John Hawkins' ship, 1587.
19. Lord Howard, 6 July 1588.
20. An expert in 1646, talking about Mercator's chart of 1569.
21. *The Calendars of State Papers.*
22. Medina Sidonia's orders to the Armada's captains, in 1588.
23. Sir Francis Drake, 1578.
24. *Naval Tracts.*
25. *Naval Tracts.*
26. Traditional, from Peter Padfield, *Armada*, p.97.
27. Sir Richard Hakluyt, *Voyages*, 1598.
28. Eyewitness report on a damaged ship of the Armada, 1588.
29. Nathaniel Butler, English sailor.
30. Cyprian Lucar, *The Art of Shooting.*
31. Cyprian Lucar, *The Art of Shooting.*
32. Sir Walter Raleigh, describing the ship *Revenge,* in 1591.

Numbers in **bold** refer to pictures.